Made in United States
North Haven, CT
19 February 2023

32842721R00063